© C.U. Chan

SABAH COLOUR GUIDE

SANDAKAN

SABAH COLOUR GUIDE

SANDAKAN

History, Culture, Wildlife and Resorts
of the Sandakan Peninsula

Wendy Hutton

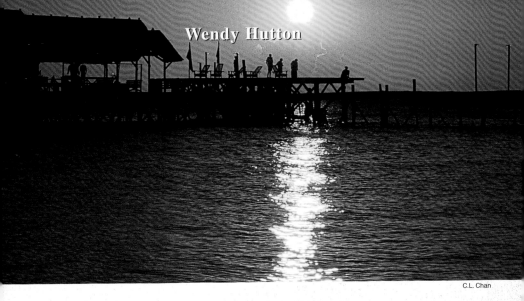

C.L. Chan

Natural History Publications (Borneo)
Kota Kinabalu
2004

Published by

NATURAL HISTORY PUBLICATIONS (BORNEO) SDN. BHD.
(Company No. 216807-X)
A913, 9th Floor, Phase 1, Wisma Merdeka
P.O. Box 15566
88864 Kota Kinabalu, Sabah, Malaysia
Tel: 088-233098 Fax: 088-240768
e-mail: chewlun@tm.net.my
Website: www.nhpborneo.com

Sabah Colour Guide: Sandakan by Wendy Hutton

ISBN 983-812-084-7

First published January 2004.

Copyright © 2004 Natural History Publications (Borneo) Sdn. Bhd.
Photographs copyright © 2004 as credited.

Printed in Malaysia.

Contents

Foreword vii

Preface viii

Message ix

Introduction 1

Precious Pearls and Gun Runners 5

Exploring Sandakan Town 23

Exploring the Region (Sepilok, Labuk

    Bay Proboscis Monkey Sanctuary

    and Lankayan Island) 53

Practical Information 73

Cede Prudente

Foreword

S andakan, located on the eastern seaboard of Sabah, is a city steeped in history. Its character is shaped by a hinterland that embodies Sabah's rich and diverse biodiversity in all its glory. With its mixture of peoples, lifestyles, cultures and faiths, Sandakan is indeed a microcosm of modern day Sabah.

With little more than an hour's journey outside this bustling port city visitors will discover forest reserves rich in wildlife, including orangutan, proboscis monkeys, brilliantly-hued birds, crocodiles and elephants. Some of Malaysia's largest wetlands teeming with wildlife also lie close to Sandakan. Just offshore from the city are the famous Turtle Islands where visitors may view rare and endangered marine turtles or indulge themselves in scuba diving. Nearby too are jungle-clad limestone outcrops with numerous caves from which birds nests have been collected for centuries.

The publication of this guide will help visitors to "discover" Sandakan and its surrounding districts. It is also another laudable contribution towards the development of tourism in the state.

Y.A.B. DATUK MUSA HAJI AMAN
Chief Minister of Sabah

PEJABAT KETUA MENTERI
TINGKAT 17 & 18, WISMA INNOPRISE, JALAN SULAMAN
88817 KOTA KINABALU
Tel: 088-429588/428233
Faks: 088-427888 E-mel: ketuamenteri@sabah.gov.my

P.K. 0054(L)-2003

Preface

by

Deputy Chief Minister
and
Minister of Resource Development and Information Technology, Sabah

For decades the capital of British North Borneo (as colonial-era Sabah was known), Sandakan attracted a great diversity of people. Vestiges of this heritage still live on in the colonial offices, houses, mosques and temples of the city, located on a magnificent deep bay with the Sulu Sea to one side and rainforests and freshwater swamps to the other.

Sandakan is famed for its orangutan sanctuary at Sepilok, and well known among locals for its inexpensive and delicious food, especially its seafood. But there is much more to be explored, both in the city and its surroundings, and this guide should prove invaluable to visitors, no matter where they come from.

Y.B. Datuk Tham Nyip Shen

Message

by

Minister of Tourism, Culture and Environment, Sabah

As the gateway to the richest concentration of wildlife in all of Borneo, Sandakan is increasingly important as a tourism destination. The city also offers an interesting insight into the history of Sabah, and with its increasing number of attractions and plans for the future, Sandakan is a place which no visitor should miss.

I welcome the publication of this guide, which follows on the success of the first book in the Sabah Colour Guide series, featuring Kudat. I feel confident that it will act as a helpful introduction to the many places of interest in and around Sandakan.

Y.B. Datuk Chong Kah Kiat

C.L. Chan

Introduction

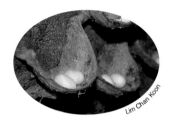

Lim Chan Koon

S andakan is one of those places whose names have a magical ring, promising all kinds of exotic surprises. The commercial centre of the large northeast district bearing the same name, Sandakan not only has an intriguing past but is the gateway to the rich wildlife of Sabah. Within less than a couple of hours of the town lies an incredible variety, both on land and in the ocean, including a forest reserve where orangutan are helped to re-adjust to life in the wild; islands where endangered marine turtles come ashore to lay their eggs; limestone caves where a rare delicacy, birds' nests, have been gathered for centuries; an island paradise in the Sulu Sea offering exciting scuba diving and Malaysia's largest freshwater swamp forest or wetlands, along the Kinabatangan river, which is teeming with wildlife.

This guide focusses on Sandakan town and the nearby Sepilok area, famed for its Orangutan Rehabilitation Centre, as well as Labuk Bay, where it is possible to view Borneo's unique proboscis monkey in a swamp setting. It also includes the resort island of Lankayan, north of Sandakan and part of the Sugud Islands Marine Conservation Area. (Separate guides in this series cover the Turtle Islands and the Kinabatangan, including Gomantong Caves.)

p. vi: The most striking feature of Berhala island, in Sandakan Bay, is its sheer red cliffs.
Above: Valuable birds nests are gathered in caves not far from Sandakan. Opposite: A newly hatched turtle swims out to sea.

C.L. Chan

C.L. Chan

C.L. Chan

C.L. Chan

C.L. Chan

Sandakan town is located near the mouth of the huge, deep Sandakan Bay, the best natural harbour in all of Borneo. To the west of the town, and spreading right down to the bay, lies the Sepilok-Kabili Forest Reserve, where the renowned Orangutan Rehabilitation Centre is located. Most of the land fringing Sandakan Bay and Labuk Bay, to the northwest, is covered with dense mangrove forests.

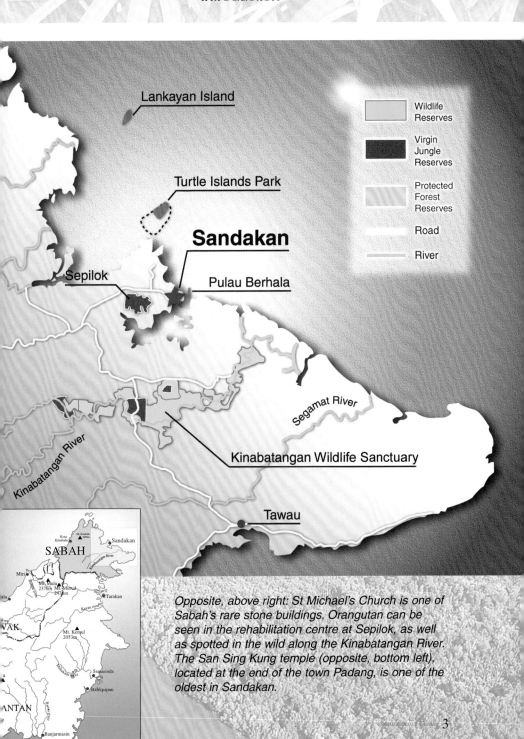

Lankayan Island

Turtle Islands Park

Sandakan

Sepilok

Pulau Berhala

Wildlife
Reserves

Virgin
Jungle
Reserves

Protected
Forest
Reserves

Road

River

Segamat River

Kinabatangan Wildlife Sanctuary

Kinabatangan River

Tawau

SABAH

Kota
Kinabalu   Mt. Kinabalu
4098m

Sandakan

Miri

Mt. Mulu
2376m   Mt. Murud
2424m

Tarakan

Kayan river

VAK

Mt. Kemul
2053m

Sarawak

ANTAN

Balikpapan

Banjarmasin

Opposite, above right: St Michael's Church is one of Sabah's rare stone buildings. Orangutan can be seen in the rehabilitation centre at Sepilok, as well as spotted in the wild along the Kinabatangan River. The San Sing Kung temple (opposite, bottom left), located at the end of the town Padang, is one of the oldest in Sandakan.

Ben Chai

Precious Pearls and Gun Runners

The early history of Sandakan is linked with that of Sulu, once an independent Muslim Sultanate whose islands dotted the waters southwest of Mindanao (now part of the Philippines). The Sultanate had long-established trading links with China and maintained a trading post in the Sandakan region, supervised by no less than one of the Sultan's sons between 1791 and 1808, a confirmation of its importance.

Sandakan and the surrounding region provided pearls, sea cucumbers, edible birds' nests, rattan, beeswax, camphor and other exotic items found in the Borneo jungles. The local chief of the trading post in the early years of the 19th century was known as Abandol, and the area protected by a small mud fort with three large guns, five small brass cannon and 60 muskets.

By the time European adventurers and merchants appeared in Southeast Asian waters, they were able to offer the Sultan an even more interesting commodity. In the 1870s, a small group of independent German and British traders established a base on Pulau Timbang in Sandakan Bay, known as Kampung German to the few fisherfolk scattered about the islands and shores of the bay. Determined to remain independent of Spain (which had colonised most of the Philippines by this stage), the Sultan of Sulu purchased arms and ammunition from one of these Kampung German traders, a Scot by the name of William Cowie. The Sultan used these arms not only to fight the Spanish, but to dispose of any local rivals.

Sulu had, by this time, become notorious for slavery, raiding the coastline of almost all of Borneo and much of Indonesia with huge boats, used to capture both male and female natives. Initially, these raiders obtained

Opposite: Downtown Sandakan sits on a narrow strip of land between the waters of the bay and a range of hills. Following pages: Downtown Sandakan in the 1930s (above). Allied bombing and deliberate Japanese destruction of the town towards the end of WWII left Sandakan in total ruins (below).

Courtesy of Sabah Museum

the natives to work as slaves for the Sultan of Sulu, but by the 19th century, the raiders had resorted to piracy, raiding, looting and terrorising the region. Naturally, this piracy was highly disruptive not only to the lives of local people but to the trade which the Europeans were attempting to establish in the area.

In 1875, an Austrian by the name of Baron von Overbeck negotiated with the Sultan of Brunei, and then in 1878, with the Sultan of Sulu, to obtain permanent ownership over what is now Sabah. He put three Englishmen in charge, and with the east coast controlled by William Pryer, he sailed off to England where he eventually sold his share in the newly created British North Borneo Company to Alfred and Edward Dent. Thus arose the strange situation of a private "chartered" company running a state, while the British government retained the right to appoint a governor.

When the new Resident, Pryer, established himself at Kampung German on Pulau Timbang in 1879, there were just 17 houses, occupied by local fishermen and three Chinese traders (thought to be Straits Chinese from Singapore, Penang or Malacca). The only other settlements in Sandakan Bay were two small fishing villages, one lived in by Bajau and the other by Suluks. In mid-June of 1879, however, Kampung German was accidentally burned to the ground, so Pryer chose the site of Buli Sim Sim, on the edge of Sandakan bay, rather than an island as the site for the new settlement.

A Hospitality All Its Own

The first capital of the newly established settlement of British North Borneo was Kudat, but in 1883, it was relocated to Sandakan. (This was due partly to a shortage of fresh water in Kudat, as well as fears of piracy.) William Pryer wasted no time in encouraging locals from villages nearby to settle in Sandakan (or, as the new settlement was briefly called, Elopura), and enterprising traders and planters, as well as coolies to work on the plantations, were welcomed.

So popular was the idea of making one's fortune in Sandakan that the population increased by around 500% in the first five years. By 1882, around 50% of Sandakan's population was Chinese, most of them from Singapore rather than Hong Kong or China. Plantations of Manila hemp (used for making rope), coffee, cocoa and coconuts were established, and traders began setting up businesses. As early as 1882, enterprising Kwan Woon Kwong established Sandakan's oldest company, Man Woo Loong, and several Hong Kong Chinese firms set up representative offices in Sandakan.

Chinese contract labourers were hired to work in the tobacco and coconut estates, but the really large influx of Chinese into Sandakan (and, indeed, other areas of Sabah) did not begin until the 1920s, when those already established were given free passage to bring in their wives and relatives. By the 1920s, the majority of Chinese settlers in Sandakan were Hakka, but the Cantonese were the next biggest group, eventually leading to Sandakan's nickname of "Little Hong Kong".

The Dutch, who were interested in establishing tobacco—which they already grew in Indonesia, then known as the Dutch East Indies—began planting in Sandakan district and by 1888, some 2,000 hectares along the lower reaches of the Kinabatangan river had been leased.

An Australian also leased a huge area of rich soil along the Kinabatangan to grow sugar cane, but just after clearing of the land had begun, the price of sugar dropped dramatically. Thus the owner of the concession, Benjamin de Lissa, abandoned his plans to plant the cane, and to cut his losses, in 1885 he shipped the timber felled during clearing to Australia.

De Lissa, however, was by no means the first timber exporter from Sandakan, for as early as 1879, a Chinese trader had already shipped sawn planks. In 1885, another Chinese merchant employed 200 men to fell timber for export, by the following year, two Sandakan-based Chinese companies were exporting wood to China.

Demand for the valuable hardwood obtained from the rainforests around Sandakan increased, shipped primarily to Hong Kong and China, where it was frequently used as sleepers for railroads and even in the construction of the Temple of Heaven in Beijing. However, until the mechanisation of the timber trade (which gathered pace in the 1960s), felling of the forest was carried out at a sustainably low level.

Fung Ming Shan, the first Kapitan China (head of the Chinese community) was appointed in 1883, and became the first Chinese to sit on the North Borneo Council. By 1908, Sandakan's Chinese community had formed the Chinese Chamber of Commerce to encourage the improvement of trade in North Borneo.

The first newspaper in the country, the *British North Borneo Herald*, began publication as a

C.L. Chan

Newly arrived Chinese quickly established temples in Sandakan.

Sandakan's Pu Ji Shiih Buddhist temple, reached via a dramatic gateway (bottom left), offers a panoramic view of the bay (opposite, top). The interior contains massive pillars (below left). The old cemetery has many Chinese graves (below), as well as a Japanese memorial. Other important temples are Pau Kung temple, opposite the Chinese quarter of Buli Sim Sim water village (below centre) and one of Sandakan's oldest temples, Sang Sing Kung (opposite below right).

Photos: C.L. Chan

monthly as early as 1883, and continued right up until the Japanese Occupation. Communication with the outside world was ensured when the telegraph connection between Sandakan and London was established in 1897, and somewhat surprisingly, perhaps, Sandakan had an automatic telephone exchange (installed in 1923) before the larger cities of Shanghai and Hong Kong.

There was very little flat land between the hills and the sea, so reclamation was begun, enabling the gradual building of many of today's downtown streets, as well as the Padang (Recreation Ground), the latter first reclaimed in 1902. At the back of the Padang, the multi-racial Sandakan Recreation Club (still flourishing) was formed the same year.

Sandakan quickly developed a small international community. There were British administrators and planters, Chinese, Arab and Indian traders, Dutch and Japanese planters, Chinese and Japanese contract workers and brothel keepers, while the local community included Orang Sungei, Ida'an, some Murut and Dusun, Bajau, Suluk and Illanun (the last three groups originally from the Philippines).

The earliest Japanese who came to Sandakan in the 1890s were mainly coolies, contract workers and prostitutes, but around 1910, Japanese investors and planters became involved in ventures in Sandakan and particularly in the far southeast of North Borneo, around Tawau. One of the most successful Japanese plantations grew jute in an estate near Kampung Bilit (upriver from Sukau along the Kinabatangan), employing 1,700 workers in 1935.

In the decade between 1910 and 1920, Sandakan had become a place where, according to Oscar Cook (*Borneo: Stealer of Hearts*) "the steamers of the World can meet. From Australia, from Manila, from China and the Dutch East Indies they come. And their coming brings a presence, breathes a wider, freer life that is felt in every corner of the town. One forgets that Europe is 9,000 miles distant or that one is living in a little known tropical Protectorate

Cede Prudente

Japanese graves (above) include that of Okuni o the South Seas (opposite, right). Some Japanese women (opposite, left), married resident Chinese

under the autocratic rule of a Chartered Company; or that the sea is full of weird delicacies beloved by the Chinese and the jungle is inhabited by elephant and rhinoceros and pig and deer... Here today and gone tomorrow: a traveller of repute, a great journalist, a naturalist, a bioscope operator, an opium smuggler—they all pass through, all come to the club; they tell their stories, and shed their personalities, leaving behind them some subtle contact of the world—the great big World that knows not Jesselton, passes by the Labuk, yet embraces Sandakan, bequeathing it a tolerance and sympathy and hospitality all its own."

The Sandakan Club provided a social centre for Europeans. Wong Sow Chuan, probably the richest man in Sandakan, opened the first hotel (which as managed by a European) in 1885 to cater to visitors. St Mary's, Sandakan's first school, was begun in 1887, with the first Chinese school, Sung Siew, founded nine years later.

Sandakan Brothel No. 8

One of the most remarkable Japanese to have lived in Sandakan was Inoshita Okuni. Born in 1849 to a very poor farming family in southern Japan, she went to Nagasaki and became the mistress of an Englishman at the age of about 15, becoming fluent in English. Eventually, after the Englishman had left and when she was around forty, Okuni decided to become a trader, going

C.L

first to Singapore and then moving on to Sandakan in the early 1890s, where she first opened a store and then a brothel known as Sandakan No. 8 (which was written about in a book and featured in a Japanese film of the same name). She was renowned for her kindness and charity to people from all walks of life, and actively encouraged a number of Japanese to settle in Sandakan or to develop coconut plantations in the district. She was widely known in Japanese communities throughout Southeast Asia as "Okuni of the South Seas". Unlike most Japanese, Okuni never wanted to return to Japan. She was responsible for building, at her own expense, the Japanese cemetery on the hills behind the town, and some years before her death, constructed her own tombstone on the site, where she was eventually buried.

Top: Berhala island, with Sandakan town seen in the background. Opposite: Poignant memorials to those who lost their lives in WWII.

By the 1930s, Sandakan had just 27 kilometres of sealed road. In the words of American writer Agnes Keith, who wrote about her life in Sabah in *Land Below the Wind*, the roads of Sandakan "might be driven around in three-quarters of an hour, with a passing glimpse of the golf club, Paupers' Home, the wireless station and the agricultural station. At one end of the road is the jungle ... at the other end is the Sandakan Club, and bachelors may be located there who will tell good elephant stories".

During WWII, Sabah was invaded by the Japanese and Sandakan captured in January 1942. The Europeans were rounded up and initially held on Pulau Berhala (a large island not far from Sandakan town which had been used as a quarantine station and a leprosy sanitarium); they were later sent to prisoner-of-war camps in Kuching.

Cede Prudente

Many of the locals, especially the Chinese, lost their lives during the Occupation. Allied forces, in an attempt to dislodge the Japanese, began bombing Sandakan in 1944, and by the time the Japanese realised the war was lost, they completed the destruction of the town by burning whatever buildings were left in 1945.

With the infrastructure left in ruins, the British North Borneo company could not afford to rebuild Sabah after the war, so it became a British colony in 1946 and the capital was moved to Jesselton (now Kota Kinabalu).

The Phoenix Arises

Rebuilding of war-damaged Sandakan was begun almost immediately after the end of the war and by the 1950s, increasing timber exports and other trade which this industry generated gave Sandakan a boom that lasted about three decades. Until 1952, the colonial British Borneo Timber Company had enjoyed a monopoly on the logging industry, but when this was lifted, several Chinese

Views of downtown Sandakan.

C.L. Chan

C.L. Chan

living in Sandakan applied for licences and began logging along the flat land of the Kinabatangan, where it was relatively easy to extract the logs.

Removal of felled timber was a slow process initially, with massive logs man-handled with wooden levers onto a cradle and hauled along a track of greased wooden poles by men in a system known as *kuda kuda* (literally "horses"). Steam engines to help the hauling were gradually introduced, and by the 1950s, tractors were beginning to be used for logging on hill slopes. The landscape around Sandakan changed dramatically as the valuable timber of the rainforest was felled. During the height of the logging boom, Sandakan town was reputed to have more millionaires per head of population than anywhere on earth. By the 1980s, areas which had once been covered by rainforest were being planted with other "green gold": oil palm plantations and, to a much lesser extent, cocoa. Sandakan town today goes about its business quietly, without the extravagance of old.

As Sandakan grew in the early years of the 20th century, it spread along the shoreline towards Pasir Putih. Although the housing and shopping complexes in places like Bandar Ramai Ramai and Hsiang Garden have a somewhat faded air today, the newer areas of Sandakan present a different and more dynamic face. Starved for space along the bay, the town eventually spilled over the ridge of hills and out to the west, into the more affluent suburbs where the majority of the population now lives.

The main road leading out of town, first known as Jalan Utara (North Road) then as Jalan Labuk, ends at the famous Mile 32, the junction of the roads to Lahad Datu and other east coast towns, and the road across to Sabah's west coast. Despite conversion to the metric system many years ago, and the use of kilometres on all the road signs, the people of Sandakan stick to the old habit of naming an area according to where it is located along the Labuk road. Thus, the town of Bandar Indah, the newest and perhaps largest development of shops, offices, restaurants and entertainment spots, is referred to by the locals as "Mile 4".

The rugged landscape of Sabah, with the mountains of the Crocker Range creating a formidable barrier between the east and west coast, ensured the relative isolation of the main settlements of Sandakan, Tawau, Kudat and Jesselton (Kota Kinabalu) for many decades. The only feasible way of getting between these towns was by sea, although eventually, an air service offered an alternative. The road to Telupid, in the interior to the west of

New shopping areas (such as "Mile 4") are growing up across the hills behind the old downtown area.

C.L. Chan

Reclamation is bringing new life as well as more land to the town. A new project is set to reclaim land in front of the current fish market, seen at bottom right, creating a new commercial and residential area.

C.L. Chan

C.L.

C.L. Chan

Cede Prudente

C.L. Chan

Sandakan, was not constructed until around 1970, and a sealed road all the way across to Kota Kinabalu not completed until the early 1990s. Today, Sandakan is linked by road to the capital, as well as to the east coast towns of Lahad Datu, Semporna and Tawau; in addition, there are frequent flights from Sandakan to the rest of the state today, making it easily accessible.

Cede Prudente

Cede Prudente

The road towards Pasir Putih passes reclaimed areas such as Bandar Ramai Ramai (opposite, above). Sandakan offers an 18-hole golf course (opposite, centre). The Clock Tower (right) is a well-known landmark, as is the old Post office (above). Although currently a town, Sandakan hopes to achieve city status in 2004; the current Town Hall is seen (above left).

C.L. Chan

C.L. Chan

The bustling market (above) and cheerful children (below). Roadside vendors (opposite) add colour and life to the town.

Tee Kim Ling

Exploring Sandakan Town

S andakan today is a town with a split personality. Downtown Sandakan, wedged onto a narrow strip of flat land between a low ridge of sandstone hills and the deep waters of the bay, looks out to sea and across to the east, where the border with the Philippines is just 30 km away.

Something of the flavour of old Sandakan lives on in the tightly packed streets where pavement vendors spread their watches, belts, CDs and sunglasses, and in the stilt villages above the sea at Buli Sim Sim. The streets around Sandakan market are filled with the tantalising fragrance of curry spices, while open-fronted restaurants tempt shoppers—whose faces and languages bear witness to their diverse origins—to pause for a drink or a quick snack before braving the nearby bus station.

C.L. Chan

The downtown area is small, the streets (especially near the market and bus station) congested, and parking difficult. Sandakanites are now looking forward to the commencement of a huge project that will revitalise the downtown area, removing the famous fish market from its current seaside location and reclaiming a large piece of land from the bay to make Harbour Square, a shopping, hotel and entertainment area.

What's in a Name?

The name "Sandakan" is derived from the Suluk words "*sanda*", meaning to pawn, with "*kan*" being the suffix. Thus, Sandakan means "the place which was pawned", although history does not tell us who pawned it or why. William Pryer, appointed Resident of the East Coast in 1879, chose the site of Buli Sim Sim as the start of a new town in Sandakan harbour, naming it

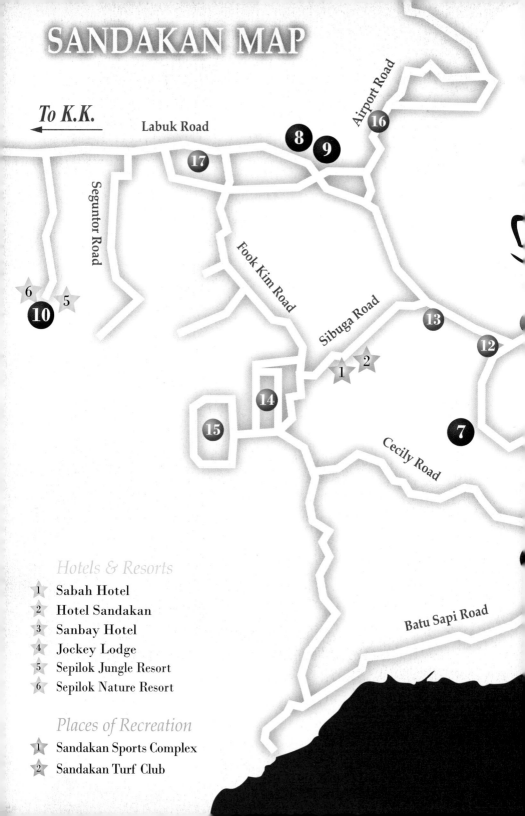

SANDAKAN MAP

To K.K.

Labuk Road

Seguntor Road

Airport Road

Fook Kim Road

Sibuga Road

Cecily Road

Batu Sapi Road

Hotels & Resorts

1 Sabah Hotel
2 Hotel Sandakan
3 Sanbay Hotel
4 Jockey Lodge
5 Sepilok Jungle Resort
6 Sepilok Nature Resort

Places of Recreation

1 Sandakan Sports Complex
2 Sandakan Turf Club

Places of Interest

1. Buli Sim Sim Water Village
2. Sandy Plain
3. Agnes Keith's House
4. Chinese & Japanese Cemetery
5. Rotary Observation Point
6. Rotary Trig Hill Tower
7. Sandakan Forest Park
8. Sandakan Crocodile Farm
9. Australian War Memorial
10. Sepilok Orangutan Rehabilitation Centre
11. English Tea House

Places of Worship

Sandakan Mosque
Sang Sing Kung Temple
Puh Ji Shiih Temple
Pau Kung Temple
Tam Kung Temple
Sri Sithi Vinayager Temple
St Michael & All Angels Church

Other Locations

1. Sandakan Town
2. Bandar Ramai-Ramai
3. Bandar Leila
4. Bandar Nam Tung
5. Bandar Tanah Merah
6. Bandar Karamunting
7. Hsiang Garden
8. Taman Grandview
9. Bandar Tong Huat
10. Bandar Kim Fung
11. Bandar Pasaraya
12. Bandar Indah
13. Taman Tshun Ngen
14. Taman Sibuga
15. Taman Mawar
16. Taman Fajar
17. Bandar Sibuga Jaya
18. Berhala Island

SANDAKAN CENTRE

To Trig Hill

Seventh Day
Adventist
Church

Basel Mission
Church

Kun
Te

St. Michael's
Secondary
School

St. Michael
Angels C

St. Mary's Church
(Roman Catholic)

Cheng Ming
School

 Bandar Ramai Ramai

Jalan Leila

Wisma

Leila Road

Sandakan
State Library

Post Office

Bestmart Supermarket

Sandakan
Community
Centre

Tun Razak
Park

Sandakan Bay

C.L. Chan

C.L. Chan

Elopura or Beautiful City. The locals continued to refer to it by the old name of Sandakan, so Elopura was eventually dropped. Somewhat surprisingly, however, during the Japanese occupation of British North Borneo, they changed the name back to Elopura. At the end of the war, however, Sandakan once again reverted to its old name.

The original site of Sandakan is **Buli Sim Sim water village**, where today, houses linked by boardwalks sit above the sea. This is no ramshackle collection of flimsy shacks but a permanent suburb of solid wooden houses with piped water and electricity. Many of the residents refuse to be tempted by the prospect of housing in apartment blocks, preferring their unique lifestyle above the sea, with its cooling breezes and gentle slap of water on the piles supporting their home. Their location is especially important to many of the men living in the Muslim section of Buli Sim Sim, who still make their living by fishing, and can literally step from their front door into their boat.

Dozens of flowering plants arranged along the boardwalks or hanging in front of the houses, flowery sarongs flapping in the wind, fish nets drying in

Cede Prudente

Ben Chai

The stilt villages of Buli Sim Sim are one of the most interesting districts to explore (opposite, below). Mosques in the old part of town and Buli Sim Sim water village (opposite, above) contrast with the shops of a new shopping district (above). Following pages: Sandakan town, viewed from the bay. Behind the range of hills is the large, shallow Labuk Bay.

the sun, and the seemingly constant presence of children make the Muslim section of the stilt village an attractive and lively place to visit. The villagers are warm and welcoming, but it is, of course, courteous to ask before taking photographs—the children, however, will probably be pleading to have their picture taken.

Further away from the seafront Sandakan District Mosque, the boardwalks—which have been referred to a *jambatan* or bridges in the Muslim quarter—suddenly become known as *lorong* or lanes. The decoration of the houses, as well as the music and language of the TV programmes changes, and with the presence of the large Pau Kung temple on the land opposite, it becomes obvious that you are now in the Chinese quarter of the stilt village.

It is fascinating to stroll the narrow boardwalks linking these houses, and to observe the lifestyle of the folks who make the stilt village their home. A seafood restaurant located at the end of Lorong E, right in front of the temple, encourages visitors to linger, and if they want to stay even longer, they can spend the night in the bed and breakfast accommodation which is part of this large Chinese family home.

The streets of **downtown Sandakan** are unromantically but logically given numbers, the four avenues or *leboh* running parallel to the waterfront

Ben Chai

crossed by streets running from the bay to the hill. The exception to this is the road in front of the markets and local bus terminus, named Jalan Pryer after the founder of Sandakan. (As a side note for those who may be interested, the famous Sandakan Brothel Number 8 was located in Lebuh Tiga, roughly on the site of today's Borneo Dispensary.)

Sandakan market spreads over several buildings along Jalan Pryer and includes a fruit and vegetable market, a dry goods market, general market and fish market. An early morning visit to the **Sandakan Fish Market** gives visitors a glimpse of the incredible variety of fish and seafood harvested from the nearby waters. All the familiar favourites are there, and sometimes esoteric species one may never have seen before, all piled into woven baskets or set in gleaming mounds on tiled benchtops, or being carted off to trucks waiting to transfer the seafood to restaurants, hotels and local markets.

Located off Leboh Empat (Fourth Avenue) on the lower slopes of the hill behind the town, the **Sandakan Tourist Information Centre** is on one side of a small square by the MPS (Sandakan Municipal Council), opposite the Police

Scenes in downtown Sandakan.

Lively scenes in the Sandakan market, a must for visitors.

Sidney Wee

Ben Chai

Ben Chai

Ben Ch

Sidney Wee

Cede P

Tee Kim Ling

Fishing boats such as these (above) bring their catch right to the seafront of the fish market. For most locals, going to the market is a chance to socialise as well as to purchase an incredible range of goods (opposite). Batu Sapi (left), a rock said to resemble a cow is near Batu Putih.

Cede Prudente

C.L. Chan

Ben Chai

Cede Prudente

M.C. Cad

Sabah Tourism Board

The Pryer Memorial (above left) is opposite the Tourist Information Centre (above). Sandakan Memorial Park is on the site of a Japanese POW camp, where many British and Australian soldiers lost their lives.

Station. A range of brochures on Sabah, as well as Sarawak and other parts of Malaysia, is available here. The building in which the information centre is located was once the main administration building of the British North Borneo Company, and the information centre itself was the Sandakan Post Office.

Opposite the Information Centre sits the **Pryer Monument,** a granite structure which once contained a drinking fountain and which was erected during the days of the Chartered Company to honour the founder of Sandakan, William Pryer.

Leading up from Leboh Empat are the **Hundred Steps** (which are multiplied ten-fold to become the Tangga Seribu or Thousand Steps in the Malay sign). These very steep steps provide a short cut to the houses perched on the hilltop (once known as Red Hill), including the Agnes Keith House, as well as to the old cemetery, but these steps are far less frequently used today than they were during the colonial period.

C.L. Chan

Above: The house of American writer Agnes Keith (right) has been rebuilt and established as a museum. Following pages: The Sabah Hotel, Sandakan's most luxurious resort, built on the site of the old colonial Sandakan Hotel.

An American writer, Agnes Keith—married to Englishman Harry Keith, Conservator of Forests, Game Warden and Director of Agriculture—wrote what became a classic book on their life in British North Borneo. *Land Below the Wind*, first published in 1939, is an affectionate, often humorous look at Sabah and its people. After their imprisonment during the Japanese occupation of WWII, the Keiths returned to Sandakan and their beloved hilltop house, which had been bombed, was re-built. Agnes Keith's book

Ben Chai

English Tea House

C.L. C

C.L.

English Tea House

The English Tea House seen from the air (opposite, top right) captures the ambience of the bygone colonial days, including croquet on the lawn (opposite, top left). The old cemetery is the final resting place of many different races, including the Chinese, whose distinctively shaped graves are seen opposite below.

of the war years, *Three Came Home*, was subsequently made into a Hollywood movie.

After more than a decade without occupants, the hilltop house on Jalan Istana was acquired and lovingly restored by the Sabah Museum. Opened as a museum, the **Agnes Keith House** contains exhibits which focus primarily on the Keiths, as well as some of the other tenants who lived there. Displays of reproduction furniture, old photographs and memorabilia, and an audio-visual display all help bring back a bygone era.

Located next to Agnes Keith's house is another beautifully restored colonial-era government house, which has a new lease of life as **The English Tea House**. Offering an unrivalled view of Sandakan and the bay, the tea house has a magnificent garden complete with a gazebo and even a croquet lawn, as well as shady dining terrace (for more, see page 82).

Until the opening of the English Tea House, the **Rotary Observation Point** immediately below offered the best place to gaze on Sandakan, together with a convenient parking spot.

The **old cemetery** overlooking Sandakan is reached via Jalan Istana and Jalan Chinese Cemetery. The final resting place of many indigenous non-Muslim Sabahans, Chinese, Indians, Filipinos, Eurasians and others, this is also the site of a number of Japanese tombs where some of the girls who worked as prostitutes in the early days of Sandakan are buried. Largest of all is the monument built well in advance of her death by Sandakan's famous owner of Brothel No. 8, Inoshita Okuni. These graves, which are difficult to locate without a guide, are found below a large memorial (built in 1989) dedicated to the Japanese who lost their lives during WWII; this is clearly visible on the right of the road near a car park.

The simplicity and restraint of the Sandakan District Mosque contrasts with the many colourful Chinese temples found in Sandakan.

One of the earliest mosques in Sandakan was built by an Indian Muslim in the 1890s. This has not survived, and the oldest mosque still standing is the **Masjid Jamek**, nestled on the hillside next to the multi-storey Wisma Sandakan in Lebuh Empat (Fourth Avenue). Although this offers a pleasantly shady verandah where the faithful can rest or even sleep when prayers are not in progress, this mosque is of no particular architectural interest.

To cater to the needs of the large Muslim population of Sandakan, a large mosque (completed in 1988) was built on the shoreline next the Kampung Buli Sim Sim. The stark simplicity of the solid grey walls and the needle-like minaret of the **Sandakan District Mosque** make it a distinctive landmark along the Buli Sim Sim Highway.

Sandakan's oldest Chinese temple, which is also perhaps the most atmospheric, is dedicated to the Goddess of Mercy. **Tokong Kun Yam**, located on the left of Jalan Singapura (Singapore Road) about 100 metres uphill from the Sandakan Recreation Club, was built in 1868; today, it sits wedged between two large wooden Chinese houses. The tiny temple—its timbers permeated with the fragrance of incense—has several small altars,

Au Kam Wah

C.L. Chan

譚公聖祖廟

公惠隱心化克元佑佑德宣
公爾在佑廣扶慈功回緣

背澤漸化照玄機扶道德緣
譚祖功扶彼玄機扶道德緒

C.L. Chan

靈光熙化顯萬有
忠氣的

C.L. Chan

廟祖聖公譚

C.L. Chan

C.L. Chan

C.L. Chan

the main one dominated by many statues of the Goddess of Mercy, some of them clothed in colourful brocade.

Contributions from Sandakan's growing Chinese community (with the exception of the Hokkiens, who built their own temple) made possible the construction of the **San Sing Kung temple** in 1885. Located at the back of the Padang, beside the Sandakan Recreation Club, this is a very active temple for it is dedicated to three saints: the saint of righteousness, the protector of sailors and fishermen, and the Min Cheong emperor, who is thought to bring luck to those sitting examinations. Not surprisingly, the temple is busier than usual during school exams. A bronze bell donated by Sandakan's first Kapitan China, Fung Ming Shan, still hangs within the temple.

Built to cater for Sandakan's Christian community, **St Michael and All Angels Church** is located on the hillside known to the colonials as Elton Hill, after the Reverend WH Elton. In 1888, Elton opened a small school which doubled as a place for prayers, until the idea of building a permanent church took hold. St Michael's is one of the very few buildings in all of Sabah to be made of stone. This, plus its Gothic-inspired architecture, makes the church look almost as if it has been transplanted from an English village.

The construction of the church (which took almost 20 years to complete) was begun in 1893, using ironwood, brick and

then stone which is reported to have come from Sim Sim. During the war-time bombing of Sandakan, the church caught fire and only the stone walls remained. The church was rebuilt and today, remains one of Sandakan's most attractive monuments. The road up the hill to the church is still referred to by many locals as Church Road, though the signpost now claims it as Jalan Puncak (Summit Road).

Undoubtedly the most impressive house of worship in Sandakan, the **Pu Ji Shiih Temple** occupies a superb hilltop location about 4 km out of town. (To get there, follow Jalan Leila to the roundabout which indicates a right turn to "Kuil Pu Chi"; the winding road leads up the hill and eventually reaches the large car park.) The location alone—with a magnificent view down over the temple's landscaped gardens to Sandakan Bay—would make it worth

Peter H.C. Kue

C.L. Chan

C.L. Chan

Tan Swee

'rudente   Cede Prudente

a visit, but the construction and decoration of the temple's interior are equally breath-taking.

Opened in 1987 after three years of construction and at a cost of around RM3 million, the temple has three massive gilded teak statues of Buddha, as well as giant standing lanterns filled with hundreds of tiny lamps decorating each side of the main altar. Thirty-four brilliant ornate pillars, writhing with painted dragons, support the roof of the vast, airy temple. With its flickering lamps, vivid colours, the movement of worshippers and the view from the entrance, the Pu Ji Shiih Temple should not be missed.

Most visitors to Sandakan and Sepilok probably prefer to see wildlife outside captivity, but those interested in a close-up look at Sabah's biggest reptile can visit the **Crocodile Farm**, located at Mile 8 on Jalan Labuk. Descendants of crocodiles once gathered wild are bred in captivity for their skin and meat in Sabah's only crocodile farm, where around 3,000 crocodiles of varying sizes are kept in tanks and shallow pools. There is also a mini zoo with several local animals and Amazonian fish weighing more than 100 kilos. There are seven feeding times daily, with a crocodile show at 11.45 am and 4 pm on weekdays, with an extra show at 2 pm on Sundays and public holidays. Call 089-660666 for more information.

Located on the site of a notorious WWII prisoner-of-war camp in what is now the suburb of Taman Rimba, about 11 km outside of Sandakan, the clearly sign-posted **Sandakan Memorial Park** is well-maintained and beautifully landscaped. The park, which includes a small museum, is a memorial to the thousands of Australian and British who lost their lives

Dominating a ridge just south of town, the Pu Ji Shiih Temple is dramatic both day and night (opposite). Crocodiles and other local animals can be seen at the Crocodile Farm (above).

C.L. Chan

C.L. Chan

C.L. Chan

L. Chan

Sandakan is well known for its wide range of delicious and inexpensive seafood, as well as excellent local vegetables.

during the Japanese occupation. The rusting remains of an excavator, a generator and a boiler still lie in their original positions, near steps leading up to a small Commemorative Pavilion.

This museum—with a stained glass window incorporating typical flowers of Sabah, Britain and Australia—contains maps, photographs and panels which relate the story of the Sandakan POW camp, and the three "death marches" to Ranau, some 260 km away through the jungle. Only six of approximately 2,400 prisoners who had survived the atrocities of the camp were alive at the end of the death marches. The courage and support of the local population, who risked their lives to help the prisoners, is also recorded in this moving museum.

Cede P●

Sandakan Memorial Park is a beautifully landscaped and well maintained memorial to prisoners of war and locals who lost their lives during WWII.

Exploring the Region

The highlight of any visit to Sandakan, the Sepilok Orangutan Rehabilitation Centre is located inside the Sepilok-Kabili Forest Reserve. Increasingly attracted by the peaceful surroundings of this beautiful location where orchards have long been established, visitors are now taking advantage of the range of accommodation located on or just off the Sepilok road. Sepilok is becoming a destination in its own right, with additional attractions currently being developed by the Forest Research Centre, and with more than just the orangutan to interest visitors to the Sepilok-Kabili Forest Reserve.

Roughly 23 km from Sandakan, the clearly sign-posted Jalan Sepilok leads directly to the **Sepilok Orangutan Rehabilitation Centre** 2.5 km away, passing the large Forest Research Centre en route. A public bus service (see details on page 75) takes visitors who are not on a tour or who do not have their own transport right to the entrance; it is also possible to take a taxi directly from Sandakan airport. (Please see page 76 for details on opening hours, feeding & video times and charges.)

The need for a sanctuary to provide a home for orangutan whose habitat had been disturbed, and for orphaned orangutan to be cared for and trained to return to the wild, was acknowledged as early as 1961. It was not until 1964, however, that the Sepilok Orangutan Rehabilitation Centre became a reality, largely due to the persistence of Barbara Harrisson (wife of the Curator of the Kuching Museum, Tom Harrisson). Funded by the Sabah government, the Centre is located within the 4,294-hectare Sepilok-Kabili Forest, a magnificent virgin rainforest that ends in mangrove swamps at the edge of Sandakan Bay.

Ben Chai

Cede Prudente

S.K Jacobson

Ben Chai

The famous Sepilok Orangutan Rehabilitation Centre, (previous pages & left) is surrounded by lush rainforest. Visitors are able to see semi-wild orangutan moving in the forest, and to observe their twice-daily feeding sessions (next page).

The gentle, red-haired orangutan, a large ape found only in Borneo and Sumatra, is endangered largely owing to loss of habitat. Orphaned babies (and, in the past, confiscated pets) are lovingly cared for at the Rehabilitation Centre. Their health is constantly monitored, and after an initial quarantine, the young animals are taught the necessary skills for survival in the wild. Without their mothers to teach them over as long as six years, these otherwise remarkable and intelligent young animals would not even learn to recognise edible food, climb safely or make the nests in which they sleep each night.

As soon as the young orangutan have developed sufficient confidence to move about outside, they are transferred during the day to an outdoor

Cede Prudente

M.C. Cadman

nursery. They learn to move through the trees twice a day to a feeding platform, where they are given bananas and milk to supplement their diet during the period they are taught to forage for wild food in the forest. Once they are mature and independent, the orangutan move off to live into the forest reserve, sometimes returning for a free meal if the supply of food in the forest is limited.

Visitors are able to take the boardwalk from the Centre's reception area through the forest to the feeding platform, where benches are arranged to form a spacious viewing area. It is not unusual for some of the more mischievous young males to approach visitors on the boardwalk; call a ranger if they decide to take an interest in your camera or handbag, as you'll never win a tug of war with these strong apes.

As feeding time approaches, the orangutan move slowly through the trees, dangling by their incredibly strong arms. Not for them the flying leaps of the proboscis monkey or the long-tailed macaques; the latter are noisy, confident creatures which hover around the feeding platform or even the

C.L. Chan

Sepilok Nature Resort, next to the Sepilok forest reserve, has a private collection of beautiful native orchids and other plants.

C.L. Chan

Ben Chai

C.L. Chan

Above & opposite: The Forest Research Centre at Sepilok.

visitors' area, in hopes of being able to steal a few bananas. The baby orangutan have winsome faces and their behaviour is so like that of their human counterparts that the temptation to cuddle them is almost irresistible. However, as human diseases (even the common cold) can be transmitted to orangutan, it is vital to keep your distance, even if they do approach.

Before going to the feeding platform, it is helpful to learn more about the orangutan and their environment by watching the video shown three times daily, and by looking through the Exhibit Centre, both located near the Reception & Ticketing area.

Several **nature trails** have been developed within the magnificent forest reserve at Sepilok. These include the 250-metre Phenology Trail, where the effects of climate on the forest and its inhabitants are interpreted. There is also the 2-km Sepilok Water Hole trail, which passes the Birder's Tower, about 1.4 km into the forest. Although it is possible to follow a 5 km-trail for about 2 hours to the mangrove forest at Sepilok Laut, where a chalet is located on the edge of Sandakan Bay, the logistics required for this trip are somewhat daunting. It is essential to obtain a permit from the Forestry Department in advance, and unless you want to return along the same route, a boat to transfer you from Sepilok Laut to Sandakan must be arranged.

It is essential to register at the Reception Centre for permission to use these nature trails, and to sign the book when you return from your walk. Do not take mosquito repellent or food with you, although a bottle of water is permitted. You can expect more than the occasional leech during the wet season (December through February), but if these are flicked off as soon as they land on you looking for a free feed, they are an annoyance rather than a problem. Unless you are familiar with the rainforest environment, you may find it useful to go with a specialised private guide to help explain the interaction of species within the forest, and to help identify the insects, birds, frogs and other creatures you may come across. It is always possible to catch sight of an orangutan, although don't count on it.

Sabah's Forestry Department maintains its large **Forest Research Centre** on Jalan Sepilok, at the edge of the Sepilok Virgin Jungle Reserve. A conservation and education facility, the Rainforest Interpretation Centre was opened in the 1990s and proved so popular that a decision was made to rebuild this on a much larger scale. As well as an enlarged Interpretation Centre, which is expected to be completed by the middle of 2004, there will be a Forestry Gallery focussing on the history of the Forestry Department

M.C. Cadman

Ben Chai

Ben Chai

Conveniently located less than an hour from Sandakan, the Labuk Bay Proboscis Monkey Sanctuary offers an excellent opportunity for close-up viewing of Borneo's most remarkable monkey.

Ben Chai

and on the forestry industry. Forest management and techniques will be incorporated in what promises to be an important facility concerning a vital aspect of Sabah.

The Sepilok Aboretum and Gardens will include a nature trail, a canopy walk over a small valley, and demonstration plots of various indigenous trees. All these features, devoted to education, research, conservation and recreation, are being developed over a ten-year period.

About another 8 km along Jalan Labuk, past the junction with Jalan Sepilok, there is a clearly marked turning which leads in along 15 km of gravel road to the **Labuk Bay Proboscis Monkey Sanctuary**. This privately owned sanctuary, located within the Yet Hing Oil Palm Estate, offers an unrivalled opportunity for close-up viewing of Borneo's unique proboscis monkeys in the wild.

Several years ago, when the owners of the estate were clearing the land for planting, they noticed a large concentration of proboscis monkeys in the mangrove forest near the edge of Labuk Bay. Rather than destroy their habitat and thus lead to the loss of these remarkable primates, the owners set aside 600 acres of land as a conservation area. During the severe El Niño-induced drought of 1997–1998, fresh water was left out for the monkeys, which slowly became more confident around humans. It was also discovered that the proboscis monkeys enjoyed eating left-over pancakes discarded by some of the estate workers, so experiments were made in feeding them.

After several years of patient effort, the proboscis monkeys have now developed the habit of dropping by the viewing lodge twice a day for a supplement to their normal diet of leaves and young shoots. Judging by the healthy condition of the monkeys and the large number of young, they flourish on this mixed diet. However, this is not something to be encouraged generally.

The monkeys start emerging from the forest an hour or so before feeding times at 11.30 am and 4.30 pm, offering superb opportunities for observing them as they play, groom each other, mate, fight or just wait about patiently. A small canal separates visitors from the proboscis monkeys, which take up positions on live trees or raised tree "stumps" artfully created from

Ben Chai

Jason Isley/Scubazoo Images

cement. But the canal does not prevent some of the bolder monkeys from approaching the viewing area on occasion, and on one famous afternoon, Zidane, a magnificent male, left his harem and climbed onto a chair on the verandah where he sat calmly next to a very important international visitor.

The male proboscis—with his enormous dangling nose, pot belly, thick white tail, reddish flat-top hairstyle and white markings which make him look as if he is wearing shorts—is one of the most remarkable creatures of Borneo. Females, much smaller and with delicate, up-turned noses, live in groups or harems with other females and their young, guarded by a dominant male. As the male monkeys mature, they join "bachelor" groups and look forward to the possibility of one day taking over a harem. All proboscis monkeys are extremely agile, making giant leaps in the trees; with their large partly-webbed hind feet, they can even swim.

The Labuk Bay sanctuary has six air-conditioned twin-sharing rooms, ideal for an overnight stay for those with an interest in bird watching as well as viewing and photographing the proboscis monkeys. (See page 75 for more details.)

Pulau Lankayan, a tear-drop in the Sulu Sea about one-and-a-half hours north of Sandakan by speed boat, is a dream come true. This small tropical island, fringed by white sandy beaches and covered with a mixture of pandanus, casuarina and other seashore vegetation, offers a Robinson Crusoe get-away with a level of comfort and cuisine that Crusoe could never have imagined.

Lankayan is part of the 46,000-hectare Sugud Islands Marine Conservation Area (SIMCA), privately managed by the owner of the resort in consultation with the Wildlife Department. This conservation

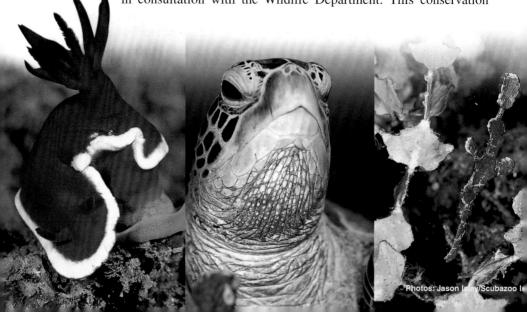

Photos: Jason Isley/Scubazoo l

C.L. Chan

Lankayan (previous pages, opposite & above), is an exquisite isle in the Sulu Sea, popular with scuba divers and vacationers.

C.L. Chan

area has been set up to restore and protect the marine life of the open seas and of the coral reefs, and to safeguard the islands which fall within the area: Lankayan, Billean and Tegaipil.

Pulau Lankayan is run as a dive resort, and as the ultimate get-away for non-divers. A second small dive resort perched on stilts over a reef near Pulau Billean is due to open by the beginning of 2004. The third island in the conservation area, Tegaipil, will be reserved for conservation activities and staff involved in managing the project.

Pulau Lankayan Resort has 16 attractive wooden chalets, all with a beach frontage, as well as comfortable rooms with verandahs and attached bathrooms in another couple of lodges. The spacious dining area adjoins a wooden sundeck jutting out over the beach, a favourite spot for relaxing and for viewing the small reef sharks which swim in at high tide for their daily meal (provided by the resort's kitchen).

Sabah's first dive resort located in the Sulu Sea (renowned for its marine biodiversity), Lankayan is known for frequent sightings of huge whale sharks

C.L. Chan

C.L. Chan

C.L. Chan

Turtle eggs are gathered and protected until the hatchlings emerge 50–60 days later. Visitors to Lankayan are able to help release the hatchlings which immediately head for the sea. Previous pages: The pure, unpolluted waters of the Sulu Sea around Lankayan island.

between March and May. It is also an important nesting sight for Green and Hawksbill Turtles.

A whole host of marine life (ranging from giant groupers to macro species such as ribbon eels) can be spotted, especially around the Lankayan wreck just a few minutes by boat from the resort's jetty. The waters around Lankayan are relatively shallow, and even non-divers can enjoy some of the marine life by snorkelling over the reef near the jetty to gaze down at the dozens of clams, whose bright purple, blue or green mantles can be seen through the crystal clear water when they open to feed.

As part of the conservation efforts practiced within SIMCA, the nesting of marine turtles is closely monitored on Lankayan. Staff patrol the beaches at night, and when female turtles come ashore to dig a nest and lay their eggs, visitors are allowed to come and watch the laying. The newly laid eggs are transferred to a hatchery to protect them from predators, and when the baby turtles emerge some 50–60 days later, guests are able to watch the hatchlings being released onto the beach in the late afternoon. The tiny turtles, with faultless orientation, race for the water and start swimming out to sea.

Dried prawns and anchovies are important ingredients in local cooking.

Ben Ch

Practical Information

HOW TO REACH SANDAKAN

There are around ten daily flights from Kota Kinabalu to Sandakan operated by Malaysia Airlines. Flight time is approximately 40 minutes, and the standard return fare RM188. Air Asia offer direct flights linking Kuala Lumpur, Malaysia's capital, with Sandakan. Air-conditioned buses leave Kota Kinabalu for Sandakan from the bus station on the road near the Padang from about 7 am daily; single fare is approximately RM30. Return buses from Sandakan leave from Mile 2.5 in Jalan Labuk from about 7.30 am daily.

TOUR OPERATORS

All major tour operators in Kota Kinabalu offer tours to Sandakan and Sepilok, as well as trips to the Kinabatangan and Pulau Selingan in the Turtle Islands. Pulau Lankayan is operated by Pulau Sipadan Resort & Tours Sdn Bhd (see page 74). Tour operators with offices in Sandakan include:

Discovery Tours
Room 908, 9th Floor, Wisma Khoo Siak Chew
Lebuh Empat, Sandakan
Tel: (089) 274106; Fax: (089) 274107; email: distours@po.jaring.my; Website: www.infosabah.com.my/discovery
Kota Kinabalu Office:
Ground Floor, Wisma Sabah
Jalan Tun Razak, Kota Kinabalu
A large tour company with their main office in Kota Kinabalu, Discovery Tours includes visits to Sepilok and Sandakan town as part of a 2-day tour with an overnight at their wildlife lodge at Sukau, on the Kinabatangan, and Gomantong Caves.

Interhighlands Adventure Sdn Bhd
Block A, Lot 4, 2nd Floor, Yuen Hup Industrial Estate
Mile 2 3/4, Jalan Labuk, Sandakan
Tel: (089) 221939; Fax: (089) 218198; Email: ihatour@tm.net.my

Run by Cede Prudente, Sabah's best nature guide and a wildlife photographer, this company specialises in wildlife viewing, bird watching and botanical excursions, as well as assisting in wildlife filming and field research. Their full-day tour of Sepilok includes watching the orangutan at feeding time, bird-watching, trail walking and observing flying squirrels at dusk. Tours to all areas of the east coast including Turtle Islands, Kinabatangan, Gomantong Caves, Tabin Wildlife Reserve and Danum Valley Conservation area are also offered.

Pulau Sipadan Resort & Tours Sdn Bhd
1st Floor, Black A, Lot 7 Bandar Pasaraya
Mile 4, Jalan Labuk, Sandakan
Tel: (089) 228081; Fax (089) 271777; Email: sepilok@po.jaring.my;
Website: www.sipadan-resort.com; www.lankayan-island.com

This company owns and manages the Sepilok Nature Resort (see Accommodation). They also arrange transport and packages to their exclusive Pulau Lankayan Island Dive Resort, north of Sandakan, as well as to their resorts on Pulau Sipadan and Mabul-Kapalai, reached via Tawau and Semporna.

SI Tours Sdn Bhd
Room 112, 1st Floor, Wisma Khoo Siak Chew
Lebuh Empat, Sandakan
Tel: (089) 213502/3, 223502; Fax: (089) 217807, 222505; Email: info@sitours.com.my; Website: www.sitours.com.my

A special interest tour company which has won several awards, SI Tours conducts nature, culture and adventure tours to all areas of interest on the east coast, including Turtle Islands, the Kinabatangan (where they maintain a riverside wildlife lodge), Gomantong Caves, Sepilok, Tabin Wildlife Reserve and Danum Valley Conservation Area; they also arrange diving tours to Sipadan, Mabul and Langkayan. Using their own fleet of boats, they conduct tours across Sandakan Bay to Kg Abai near the mouth of the Kinabatangan, and also offer seafood restaurant and B & B accommodation in the Chinese quarter of Sandakan's water village.

Wildlife Expeditions
Room 903, 9th Floor, Wisma Khoo Siak Chew, Sandakan
Tel: (089) 219616; Fax: (089) 274331; Email: sliew@pc.jaring.my: Website:
www.wildlife-expeditions.com
Kota Kinabalu Office:
331B, 3rd Floor, Wisma Sabah
Jalan Tun Razak
Tel: (088) 246000; Fax: (088) 231758 ; Email: leegn@pc.jaring.my

The longest established tour operator in Sandakan, Wildlife Expeditions specialises in nature travel and arranges trips to Sepilok, day or night tours of Sandakan, and an afternoon cruise to view the wildlife along the rivers threading through mangrove forest off Sandakan Bay. They also arrange tours to Turtle Islands, and maintain a lodge on Libaran Island nearby. Wildlife Expeditions specialised in trips to Gomantong Caves and the Kinabatangan, where they have their own lodge at Sukau.

TRANSPORT AROUND SANDAKAN

Taxis are plentiful and can be hailed in the street; they are not metred, so negotiate the fare with the driver before starting; fares in the downtown area are generally RM2–5.

Buses to Sepilok (RM1.80 one way) depart from the local bus station in Jalan Pryer, on the seafront to one side of the general market, leaving roughly on the hour. Look for buses with the destination "Batu 14" (Mile 14) run by the Labuk Road Bus Company or the Sibuga Bus Company. Take a bus departing Sandakan at 8 am to be sure to be in plenty of time for the morning feeding at Sepilok Orangutan Rehabilitation Centre. The last bus from Sepilok back to town leaves around 4.30–4.45 pm.

CONTACT DETAILS, OPENING HOURS AND FEES

Labuk Bay Proboscis Monkey Sanctuary
Yet Hing Oil Palm Estate, off Jalan Labuk at 31.5 km, opposite Consolidated Farm.
Tel: (089) 672133, 672177; Handphone (019) 853 4098, (019) 813 9717; Fax (089) 531189

Ben Chai

Approximate Feeding Times 11.30 am and 4.30 pm. Fees: RM80 non-Malaysians, including transfers; drive in RM60; RM35 Malaysians, including transfers; drive in RM15. Overnight accommodation and 3 meals, including transfers and wildlife viewing, costs RM250 per person for non-Malaysians; RM120 for Malaysians.

Sandakan Crocodile Farm
Mile 8, Jalan Labuk
Tel: (089) 660666
There are 7 feeding times daily, at 9.30 am, 11 am, 12.15 pm, 1.45 pm, 2.30 pm, 3.30 pm & 4 pm. There is a crocodile show at 11.45 am and 4 pm on weekdays, with an extra show at 2 pm on Sundays and public holidays.

Sepilok Orangutan Rehabilitation Centre
Jalan Sepilok, off Jalan Labuk
Tel: (089) 531180; Fax (089) 531189; Email: soutan@pc.jaring.my
The security gate to the Centre is open daily from 8 am until 4.30 pm, with the cafeteria also open from 8 am. The Reception and Ticketing Counter Centre is open from 9 am–11 am, and 2 pm–3.30 pm daily. The Exhibition Hall opens from 8.30 am–12.30 pm, and 2 pm–4 pm daily. Video shows are given from 8.40 am–9.10 am, 10.40 am–11.10 am, and from 3.30 pm–4 pm daily. The entrance fee (which entitles visitors to spend an entire day at the Centre, observing both feeding sessions and including taking forest trails) is RM30 for non-Malaysians, RM15 for Malaysians. A fee of RM10 is charged for still and video cameras.

ACCOMMODATION IN SANDAKAN

Sabah Hotel
1 km Jalan Utara, Sandakan
Tel: (089) 213299; Fax: (089) 271271; email: shsdksm@tm.net.my
Built on the site of Sandakan's first hotel, this attractive 4-star resort hotel is set in a backs on a lush landscaped garden surrounded by forested hills. Rooms have all modern facilities including mini-bar and tea & coffee making facilities. Recreational options include large swimming pool, gym, tennis, squash, darts and snooker. Western and Chinese cuisine, music lounge, tour desk and gift shops all available.

Photos: M.C. Cadman

Hotel Sandakan
Leboh Empat (Fourth Avenue), Sandakan
Tel: (089) 221122; Fax: (089) 221100; Email: tengis@tm.net.my Website: www.relaz.com/hotelsandakan
The newest hotel conveniently located in downtown Sandakan, this 3-star property has comfortable guest rooms. The coffee house offers international and local cuisine, with Cantonese and Sichuan favourites plus *dim sum* featured in the Palm Garden; Japanese cuisine is available in the Kon Japanese Restaurant, while there is also a bar lounge with live music. Rates range from RM173 S/RM196 D.

Sanbay Hotel
Mile 1 1/4, Jalan Leila
Tel: (089) 275000; Fax: (089) 275575; Website: www.sanbay.com.my Email: sanbay@po.jaring.my
A medium-sized 3-star hotel in a quiet location about 5 minutes from the centre of town.

Hotel NAK
Postal Address: P.O. Box 761, 90708 Sandakan.
Location: 29, Jalan Pelabuhan Lama
Tel: (089) 272988
A budget hotel right in the centre of town.

Hotel City View
Leboh Tiga (Third Avenue), Sandakan
Tel: (089) 271122; Fax: (089)273112
Popular with budget travellers, and conveniently located in Sandakan's busiest road, this hotel offers rooms at RM75 nett S/D.

ACCOMMODATION IN SEPILOK

Sepilok B & B
Off Jalan Sepilok (on road to Forestry Research Centre Arboretum & Gardens)
Tel: (089) 532288; Fax: (089) 217668
The first B & B accommodation built in Sepilok, this is also the furthest from the Orangutan Rehabilitation Centre. It is in a peaceful location, but has seen better days.
Rates are RM45 for a double room with attached bathroom; RM20 for a bed in a dormitory, including breakfast.

M.C. Cadm

Sepilok Jungle Resort
Off Jalan Sepilok
Tel: (089) 533031; Fax (089) 533029;
Email: sepilokjr@yahoo.com;
Website: www.borneo-online.com.my/sjungleresort
Located off a small road to the left about 75 metres before the entrance to the Orangutan Rehabilitation Centre, this popular family-run resort is set in luxuriant gardens with fruit trees, flowering shrubs, unusual tropical plants and meandering lakes. The Resort offers a range of accommodation to suit all budgets, from comfortable fan-cooled dormitories (with only 4 beds per room) and camping sites to deluxe air-conditioned rooms. There are conference facilities and a popular, open-sided restaurant, the Banana Cafe,

which also caters to non-guests. Warm, friendly service; free pick-up from the main road to Sandakan (Jalan Labuk) if guests telephone from the shop near the corner of Sepilok Road. Rates from RM20 to RM120, including breakfast. Internet access, TV lounge and tours arranged.

C.L. Chan

M.C. Cadman

Sepilok Nature Resort
Jalan Sepilok
Tel: (089) 228081, 535001;
Fax: (089) 217777, 535002
Email: sepilok@po.jaring.my;
Website: www.sipadan-resort.com

Located on the right of the road to the Orangutan Rehabilitation Centre, about 75 metres from the entrance, this is the most luxurious resort in Sepilok. A total of 17 wooden chalets topped with ironwood shingles are set in landscaped gardens around a lake; the beautiful tropical gardens (which back right on to the forest) are renowned for containing over 150 species of orchid. This is a particularly peaceful setting offering good opportunities for bird watching and even the bonus of possible sightings of orangutan in the nearby trees. All twin-bed chalets are air-conditioned and comfortably furnished. The restaurant is located in a magnificent timber building with massive hardwood pillars. Chalets are RM200 per night; meals range from RM15 for American breakfast to RM28 for dinner.

Sepilok Resthouse
Jalan Sepilok Tel: (089) 534900; Email: imejbs@tm.net.my

Located right next to the entrance of the Orangutan Rehabilitation Centre, this attractive 2-storey resthouse was built for the exclusive use of researchers and others working for the Wildlife Department. It is now run as a small private hotel, with 6 twin rooms and two 4-bed dormitories; there is a pleasant lounge with TV and internet, with meals available for both guests and visitors. Tours arranged. Very popular, so booking strongly advised. RM65 for an air-conditioned room; RM45 for a fan-cooled room, including breakfast.

M.C. Cadman

WHERE TO EAT IN SANDAKAN

Reflecting its diverse population, Sandakan town offers a wide range of food, from Chinese to local Muslim, Indian, Indonesian and Western fastfood, as well as excellent seafood. There are dozens of modest coffee shops and open-fronted restaurants, as well as air-conditioned restaurants (especially in the hotels). Some of the more interesting options include:

Kedai Kopi Shin Cheong Loong, in Leboh Tiga (Third Avenue) opposite the Alliance Bank, is reputedly Sandakan's oldest restaurant. It is a small, unpretentious open-fronted place and is famous for its excellent steamed fish (splashed with a little boiling oil) and chicken rice.

Ocean King Seafood Restaurant
Jalan Batu Sapi (4.5 km), Pasir Putih
Tel: (089) 618111, 616048

It's hard to miss this large, relatively new restaurant built on stilts over the bay. Just follow Jalan Leila out of town towards Pasir Putih (signposted at each roundabout), a small beach where older seafood stalls have long been popular. Ocean King has 100 tables, some of them in a large dining hall, while the more attractive location is the large covered verandah overlooking the bay towards Sandakan town, and which catches any passing breeze. There is a vague menu/price list written on a board on the verandah, but basically, if it swims you can order it. Fish, crabs, prawns, lobster, squid and various shellfish are all available and you can ask for advice on how they are best cooked. The bean curd and vegetable dishes are good, and the prices surprisingly modest. Open daily from 10 am until midnight.

Kedai Ang Ban Guan
Jalan Buli Sim Sim

This unprepossesing wooden restaurant located near the mosque at Buli Sim Sim has the reputation of serving some of the best seafood in Sandakan. Open for lunch and dinner.

Penang Curry House
Lebuh Dua (Second Avenue), next to the AM Finance

Featuring Southern Indian cuisine, including curries, *murtabak*, *roti canai* (flaky bread) and *dosay* (rice-flour and lentil pancakes), this busy open-fronted restaurant has tasty food at reasonable prices, with plenty of vegetarian options. Ice yoghurt drink (*lassi*) is also available.

Cherokee Rose Restoran
Dato Building, Kampung Garam,
Jalan Leila , Sandakan.
Tel: (089) 214746

Chinese restaurant renowned for its seafood.

Heng Loong Restaurant
Lot 28, Block 4, Bandar Pasaraya, Mile 4,
PO Box 92, PPJU Mile 1 1/2, 90307 Sandakan.
Tel: (089) 211023, 211263 Fax: (089) 273609

One of biggest Chinese restaurants in town, popular for functions, this offers a wide selection of mostly Cantonese cuisine..

New Century Restaurant
Block C, T-B
Mezzanine Lot 3,
Kedai Taman Grandview,
Jalan Buli Sim-Sim, 90000 Sandakan.
Tel: (089) 217517

Air-conditioned Chinese restaurant on the hills overlooking Sandakan Bay.

Restoran Habeeb
There are at least 8 restaurants in this chain featuring Indian and local Muslim cuisine. One of the most convenient is located directly in front of the major shopping complex, Wisma Sandakan, in Leboh Empat (Fourth Avenue). Rice (including *biryani*), *roti canai* and a wide range of ready cooked meat, fish and vegetable dishes available.

Sandakan Recreation Club
Jalan Singapura, at the end of the Padang

One of the most popular places in downtown Sandakan for Chinese food is the air-conditioned restaurant located on the 1st floor of the Sandakan

Recreation Club. Open to the public as well as members from 11 am–2 pm, and 5–10 pm daily, there is no written menu but the captain is happy to recommend dishes. It's even possible to try crocodile meat from the local crocodile farm, stir-fried with ginger and spring onion. Moderately priced.

Restoran Golf View
Seafood Steamboat Restaurant
(Hill Top Driving Range) Mile 5, Jalan Sibuga

Next to the Sandakan Golf Club, this popular open-air restaurant is famous for its steamboat, a type of foundue, and offers very good value for a wide range of food.

The English Tea House & Restaurant
Jalan Istana

Arguably more stylish and elegant than it was in its original days, an old government house next to the Agnes Keith House has been transformed into a tea house and restaurant, set in a large garden with landscaped lawns. Traditional English food is featured, as well as several Asian dishes and a range of fine teas, wines and other beverages. Traditional morning and afternoon teas, complete with cucumber sandwiches and scones with clotted cream or an Asian Tiffin, are popular. Call (089) 222544 for information or reservations.

WHERE TO EAT IN SEPILOK

Kafeteria Sepilok
The best place for inexpensive Western food such as sandwiches, salads and omelettes, as well as a few simple local dishes, ice-cream and drinks, the cafeteria is conveniently located next to the registration building within the Sepilok Orangutan Rehabilitation Centre. Open from 8 am (ideal for breakfast) until 4 pm daily.

Banana Cafe in the Sepilok Jungle Resort is an open-sided, fan-cooled pavilion overlooking a lake in a gorgeous garden setting, 10–15 minutes walk from the Orangutan Rehabilitation Centre. Moderately priced special set meals are available, while an adequate range of local and Western dishes can be ordered from the menu. Several brands of cold beer are available.

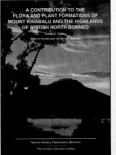

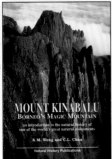
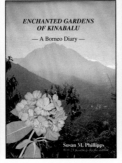

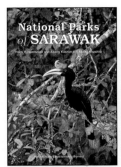

National Parks
of SARAWAK
Hans P. Hazebroek and Abang Kashim bin Abang Morshidi

A Walk through the
LOWLAND RAIN FOREST
of Sabah

Elaine J.F. Campbell

PREFERRED CHECK-LIST OF
SABAH TREES
Third Edition
Y.F. LEE

Natural History Publications (Borneo)

THE LARGER FUNGI
OF BORNEO
David N. Pegler

Natural History Publications

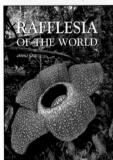

RAFFLESIA
OF THE WORLD
JAMILI NAIS

PITCHER-PLANTS
OF BORNEO
Anthea Phillipps and Anthony Lamb

*with watercolour paintings by Susan M. Phillipps
and a Foreword by Tan Jiew Hoe*

NEPENTHES
of BORNEO
CHARLES CLARKE

Natural History Publications

A GUIDE TO THE
Pitcher Plants
of Sabah
Charles Clarke

Natural History Publications (Borneo)

A GUIDE TO THE
Pitcher Plants of
Peninsular Malaysia
Charles Clarke

Natural History Publications (Borneo)

NEPENTHES
OF SUMATRA
AND PENINSULAR MALAYSIA
Charles Clarke

Natural History Publications (Borneo)

ORCHIDS
of SARAWAK
TEOFILA E. BEAMAN, JEFFREY J. WOOD,
REED S. BEAMAN AND JOHN H. BEAMAN

Natural History Publications (Borneo)
in association with
The Royal Botanic Gardens, Kew

ORCHIDS
of SUMATRA
J.B. Comber

Natural History Publications (Borneo)
in association with
The Royal Botanic Gardens, Kew

DENDROCHILUM
OF BORNEO
Jeffrey J. Wood

Natural History Publications (Borneo)
in association with
The Royal Botanic Gardens, Kew

THE PLANTS *of*
MOUNT KINABALU
3. GYMNOSPERMS AND NON-ORCHID MONOCOTYLEDONS

John H. Beaman and Reed S. Beaman

Natural History Publications (Borneo)
in association with
The Royal Botanic Gardens, Kew

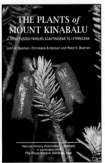

THE PLANTS *of*
MOUNT KINABALU
4. DICOTYLEDON FAMILIES ACANTHACEAE TO LYTHRACEAE

John H. Beaman, Christiane Anderson and Reed S. Beaman

Natural History Publications (Borneo)
in association with
The Royal Botanic Gardens, Kew

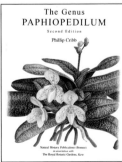

The Genus
PAPHIOPEDILUM
Second Edition
Phillip Cribb

Natural History Publications (Borneo)
in association with
The Royal Botanic Gardens, Kew

SLIPPER ORCHIDS
OF BORNEO
Phillip Cribb

Natural History Publications

THE GENUS
COELOGYNE
A SYNOPSIS

Dudley Clayton

Natural History Publications (Borneo)
in association with
The Royal Botanic Gardens, Kew

GINGERS
of PENINSULAR MALAYSIA
AND SINGAPORE
K. Larsen, H. Ibrahim, S.H. Khaw and L.G. Saw

Natural History Publications (Borneo)

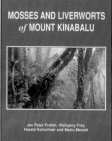

MOSSES AND LIVERWORTS
of MOUNT KINABALU

Jan Peter Frahm, Wolfgang Frey,
Harald Kürschner and Mario Menzel

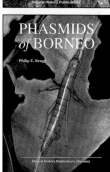

PHASMIDS
of BORNEO

Philip E. Bragg

Natural History Publications (Borneo)

An Illustrated Guide to the
STICK AND LEAF INSECTS
of Peninsular Malaysia and Singapore
FRANCIS SEOW-CHOEN

Natural History Publications (Borneo)

A GUIDE TO THE
DRAGONFLIES
OF BORNEO
THEIR IDENTIFICATION AND BIOLOGY

A.G. ORR
including photographs by
M. Hämäläinen

Natural History Publications (Borneo)

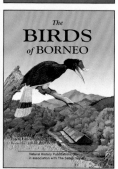

The
BIRDS
of BORNEO

Natural History Publications (Borneo)
in association with The Sabah Society

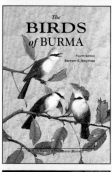

The
BIRDS
of BURMA

Fourth Edition
Bertram E. Smythies

Natural History Publications (Borneo)

Swiftlets of Borneo
BUILDERS OF EDIBLE NESTS
Lim Chan Koon and Earl of Cranbrook

Natural History Publications (Borneo)

The Natural History of
ORANG-UTAN
Elizabeth L. Bennett

Natural History Publications (Borneo)

PROBOSCIS MONKEYS
OF BORNEO

Elizabeth L. Bennett and Francis Gombek

A Field Guide to the
FROGS OF BORNEO

Robert F. Inger
Robert B. Stuebing

The Natural History of
AMPHIBIANS AND REPTILES
IN SABAH

Robert F. Inger and Tan Fui Lian

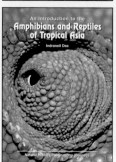

An Introduction to the
Amphibians and Reptiles
of Tropical Asia
Indraneil Das

Natural History Publications (Borneo)

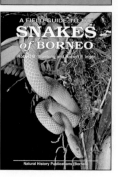

A FIELD GUIDE TO THE
SNAKES
of BORNEO
Robert B. Stuebing and Robert F. Inger

Natural History Publications (Borneo)

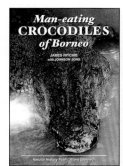

Man-eating
CROCODILES
of Borneo
JAMES RITCHIE
with JOHNSON JONG

Natural History Publications (Borneo)

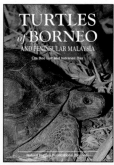

TURTLES
of **BORNEO**
AND PENINSULAR MALAYSIA
Lim Boo Liat and Indraneil Das

Natural History Publications (Borneo)

MARINE FOOD FISHES
AND FISHERIES
OF SABAH
Chin Phui Kong

Natural History Publications

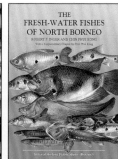

THE
FRESH-WATER FISHES
OF NORTH BORNEO
ROBERT F. INGER AND CHIN PHUI KONG
With a Supplement Chapter by Chin Phui Kong

Natural History Publications (Borneo)

LAYANG LAYANG
A Drop in the Ocean
Nicolas Pilcher, Steve Oakley and Ghazally Ismail

Natural History Publications (Borneo)

**THREE
CAME HOME**
Agnes N. Keith

Natural History Publications

Land Below The Wind
Agnes Newton Keith

Natural History Publications (Borneo)

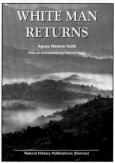

WHITE MAN
RETURNS
Agnes Newton Keith
With an Introduction by Patricia Regis

Natural History Publications (Borneo)

WITH THE WILD MEN OF
BORNEO
Elizabeth Mershon

Natural History Publications (Borneo)

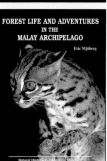

FOREST LIFE AND ADVENTURES
IN THE
MALAY ARCHIPELAGO
Eric Mjöberg

Natural History Publications (Borneo)

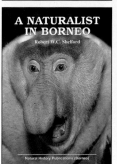

A NATURALIST
IN BORNEO
Robert W.C. Shelford

Natural History Publications (Borneo)

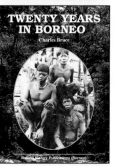

TWENTY YEARS
IN BORNEO
Charles Bruce

Natural History Publications (Borneo)

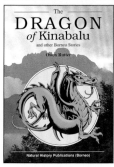

The
DRAGON
of Kinabalu
and other Borneo Stories
Owen Rutter

Natural History Publications (Borneo)

A CULTURAL HERITAGE OF NORTH BORNEO
Animal Tales
of Sabah
P. S. Shim
with illustrations by Yong Kee Hyun

Natural History Publications (Borneo)

Kadazan
Folklore
Compiled and edited by
Rita Lasimbang
Illustrated by
Suzie Majikol

Natural History Publications (Borneo)

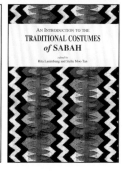

AN INTRODUCTION TO THE
TRADITIONAL COSTUMES
of SABAH
edited by
Rita Lasimbang and Stella Moo-Tan

Sabah Tourism Board
51 Jalan Gaya, 88000 Kota Kinabalu, Sabah, Malaysia
Tel: 6088-212121 Fax: 6088-212075
Email: info@sabahtourism.com Website: www.sabahtourism.com

Deluxe Room

Banquet

Amadeus

Swimming Pool

... where splendours of nature and luxury and comfort are yours!

Sabah Hotel
Sandakan

Km 1, Jalan Utara,
P. O. Box 275, 90703 Sandakan, Sabah, Malaysia.
Telephone: (6089) 213 299   Fax: (6089) 271 271
Website: www.sabahhotel.com.my   Email: shsdksm@tm.net.my
Owner: Sabah Hotel Sdn. Bhd. (Co. No. 106699-D)

EXPERIENCE THE WONDERS OF NATURE IN SOME OF THE WORLD'S BEST RAIN FORESTS AND REEFS

Serene surroundings of accommodation (top) from which nature excursions are organized to the famed Sepilok Orangutan Rehabilitation Centre, and dive Lankayan (bottom), Paradise Island of the Sulu Sea and a jewel in the Sugud Islands Marine Conservation Area.
To savour these, contact us at Tel: 6089-228081; 765200
e-mail: lankayan@tm.net.my; psrt@po.jaring.my

Sepilok Jungle Resort

Sepilok Jungle Resort is located in a more than 8 thousand acres of tropical rain forest in Sandakan, Sabah, Malaysian Borneo and is just less than 5 minutes walk from the world renowned Sepilok Orangutan Rehabilitation Centre.

This Resort provides great spots for bird watching enthusiasts.

The Resort with its tranquillity and peace is a perfect place for guests who wish to get away from "it all" to spend holidays with family and friends. It is set admist a 30 acres stunning garden with tropical fruit trees. We offer friendly and comfortable home with 57 rooms for everybody at an affordable price starting from RM18.00 nett per person inclusive of breakfast, to RM120.00 nett per air-conditioned room. Executive Room with private balcony, set admit nature with its charm and mysticism is also available.

Facilities:
Free Labuk/Sepilok Road junction pick-up; Restaurant opens daily from 7am to 10pm
Beautiful garden setty & pavilions; Shuttle service to airport & Sandakan town; Lagoons for boating and fishing; Camping ground; Laundry service; Internet service; Travel and tours; Barbecue pits; Function hall; Hot shower; And more …

SEPILOK JUNGLE RESORT
KM22, Labuk Road, Sandakan, Sabah, Malaysia.
Tel: (++6 089) 533031; 533041; 533051 Fax: (++6 089) 533029
Email: sepilokjr@yahoo.com
Homepage : www.borneo-online.com.my/sjungleresort